Sidereal
HARMONY

Relating the Circle of Fifths to the Wheel of the Zodiac

MICHAEL BANK

ISBN: 978-1-4834-3330-1 (sc)
ISBN: 978-1-4834-3329-5 (e)

Lulu Publishing Services rev. date: 6/22/2015

To Jaki Byard and Geoffrey Chaucer
for their inspiration

ACKNOWLEDGMENTS

Thank you, Dr. Edward Mario Covelli, Tony Barrett, D.B. Rielly, Matthew Barry Smith, and Kelly David Friesen, for your help, knowledge, talent, and support.

INTRODUCTION

Every diagram, system of numbers, every scheme
of harmony, and every law of the movement of the
stars ought to appear one to him who studies rightly.
—Nicomachus, *Introduction to Arithmetic*,
circa AD 100

Every time we look at a piano keyboard, on some level we are aware
of its repetitive structure. We see white keys and black keys, the
latter clustered in alternating groups of two and three. Just to the
left of any two note group of black keys, we find one of the white
keys called C. As we move rightward sequentially from any C on
the white keys, we sound the seven notes of the C major scale before
arriving at the next C. The span from the starting C to the second
one is defined as an octave.

The keyboard consists of a series of these octave units. The
octave beginning on C contains seven white keys. When sequentially
played, they lead us to a new C and the beginning of a new octave.
This is similar to the numbering of days in the week; the seven days
of the week, beginning on Sunday, transpire sequentially and lead
us to the next Sunday and a new week.

The piano's keyboard structure yields a second interesting
correlation to the way we number units of time. If one begins at a C
and moves rightward, playing the next adjacent key, white or black,
one moves through twelve keys before arriving at another C. This
sequence of sounding the twelve notes in the octave and arriving at

a new C in a new octave is similar to traversing the twelve months of a year, starting in January and arriving at a new January in a new year. As the layout of the piano keyboard is a reflection of the general structure of music, I am sure most inquisitive musicians have pondered these analogies between the way we order musical notes and the way we order units of time.

The division and measurement of time throughout history has been related to the study of the stars and planets. The seven days of the week were numbered and named after the visible ancient planets. These were the moon (Monday, or *Lunes* in Spanish), Mars (Tuesday, or *Martes* in Spanish), Mercury (Wednesday, or *Miercoles* in Spanish), Jupiter (Thursday, or *Jueves* in Spanish), Venus (Friday, or *Viernes* in Spanish), Saturn (Saturday, or *Sabado* in Spanish), and the sun (Sunday, or *Domingo* in Spanish).

Ancient astronomers divided the year into twelve months, each approximately the length of a lunar cycle. The months were correlated to the twelve signs of the zodiac. The signs of the zodiac are the constellations that lie in the ecliptic, the path of the sun in the sky. These signs divide that path into twelve equal regions, which were used to follow the seasons of the year.

The wheel of the zodiac can be drawn as a circle. Beginning with Aries in the nine o'clock position and proceeding counterclockwise sequentially, the signs of the zodiac occupy equal segments of the circumference until 360 degrees are traversed and the cycle begins again. In the same way, the twelve chromatic notes of the octave can be plotted on a circle. Starting with C at the twelve o'clock position and moving clockwise so that the next note is a fifth above its predecessor, the circle of fifths is drawn. The circle of fifths is a powerful figure in demonstrating the intrinsic symmetry and beauty in music. Thus both music and astronomy utilize circles divided into twelve sections.

The link between music and astronomy has been pondered since the sixth century BC. The Greek philosopher Pythagoras, who discovered the mathematical relations between the lengths of vibrating strings and the production of harmonious tone combinations, postulated that the movement of the heavens generated a "music of the spheres." This idea has remained largely conceptual, although many great minds have endeavored to describe the system in more mathematical detail. For example, in 1619, Johann Kepler published *Harmonies of the World*, which included chapter titles such as "The Musical Modes or Tones Have Somehow Been Expressed in the Extreme Planetary Movements." Although he went on to discover the mathematical laws that described these movements to a remarkably accurate degree, his work relating them to music has not been widely built upon.

Since the supremely rational mind and scientific vigor of Kepler did not succeed in defining a lasting link between astronomy and music, perhaps a less rational, less scientific approach is in order.

Apart from our rational faculties, humans are endowed with emotions and collective ideas that are not based on definitive logic. The full spectrum of human emotional responses can be evoked by music, and this effect is powerful, mysterious, and inexplicable. Similarly, astrology, the sister of astronomy, encompasses mythological and nonscientific ideas regarding the qualities associated with and evoked by the planets. Perhaps it is possible to correlate the affective, extrarational characteristics evoked by music with the astrological, mythological qualities attributed to the planets and then bring these associations back into a rational framework for analysis. In this way, a bridge might be formed between these two areas of human experience through mapping the visual representations of the wheel of the zodiac and the circle of fifths to each other. Once this bridge is built, moving along the known byways of these two territories may yield new insights, not only concerning music and the stars but also ourselves.

CHAPTER 1

Harmony for the Nonmusician

Music is more important than most people know.
—Jaki Byard

Since the goal of this book is to relate the wheel of the zodiac to the circle of fifths, I will first provide some background regarding harmony so that the reader can understand the derivation of this diagram and key signatures. To understand some of the material presented later in this book, I would suggest consulting *Orem Harmony Book for Beginners* or a similar text.

Harmony is defined as the combination of tones, or musical sounds. On the piano keyboard, the letter C is assigned to the white note found just to the left of any two-note group of black notes (see Figure 1). There are seven different Cs found on the standard piano keyboard, including the last key at the right end of the keyboard. Each pair of consecutive Cs defines an octave, which is named for the grouping of eight white keys between them. If two Cs are sounded on the piano in different octaves, the one on the right will have a higher pitch. *Pitch* is the highness or lowness of a tone and relates to the frequency of the sound waves produced by an instrument.

FIGURE 1

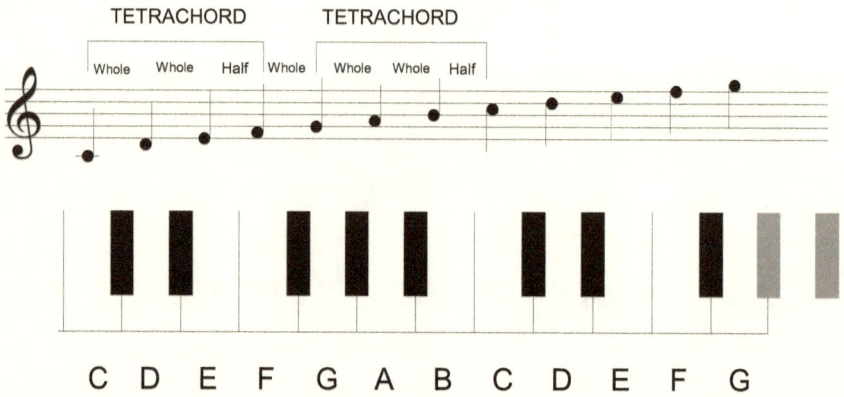

The C major scale within one octave is found by starting at a C and moving to the right, one white key at a time, until one arrives at the next C. It consists of the tones C, D, E, F, G, A, B, and C (Figure 1). The definition of a scale is a succession of tones arranged in regular ascending or descending order. There are many different scales, but we will only concern ourselves with the eight-note major scale in this chapter.

In western classical music, twelve tones are employed. These are represented on the keyboard by the seven unique white keys of the octave, C, D, E, F, G, A, and B, and the five additional black keys between C–D, D–E, F–G, G–A, and A–B (Figure 1). The smallest difference in pitch found on the piano is a half step (also known as a semitone). This difference can be found between two adjacent white keys with no black key between them, such as E–F, or, more commonly, between a white key and an adjacent black key. A whole step, or whole tone, is equivalent to two half steps, such as from C to D, which is made up of the half step from C to the black note between C and D and the half step from that black note to D.

The structure of the C major scale can be evaluated by looking at the half-step and whole-step relations between its notes. If we look at the spaces between the adjacent white keys in this scale, we see that some have an intervening black note between them (such as C–D) and others (such as E–F) do not. The white keys with a black key between them have a difference of a whole step, and the white keys that lie directly next to each other without a black key are a half step apart (Figure 1).

Looking at the first part of the C major scale, we see that C–D and D–E are whole steps, E–F is a half step, and F–G is a whole step. In the last four notes, G–A and A–B are whole steps, and B–C is a half step. So the entire C major scale is made up of five whole steps and two half steps in the following order: whole step, whole step, half step, whole step, whole step, whole step, half step. We can introduce parentheses as follows.

(whole step, whole step, half step) between C, D, E, and F

whole step between F and G

(whole step, whole step, half step) between G, A, B, and C

Here we see that the major scale can be divided into two equal groups of four successive tones, or tetrachords. In the major scale, both tetrachords (C + D + E + F and G + A+ B+ C) consist of four notes with the whole step, whole step, half step differences between them. Thus we see that the C major scale is comprised of two similar tetrachords separated by a whole step.

The major scale can begin on any of the twelve notes. The letter with which a scale begins and ends is called the tonic, or key note. In the C major scale, C is the tonic or key note.

The circle of fifths (Figure 2), as the name implies, utilizes the interval of a perfect fifth in its construction. If we count to five on the white keys moving to the right, beginning at C with each count, we sound C, D, E, F, and G. The space, or interval, between C and G is a fifth, in which G is a fifth above C. A fifth is made up of the sum of whole step, whole step, half step, and whole step, which is equivalent to seven half steps. Similarly, if we move from the C to the left the same distance, we descend via C, B, A, G, and F. In this case, we arrive at the note F, a fifth (seven half steps) below C. Looking at the circle of fifths, we see that each entry moving clockwise is the note that is a fifth above its predecessor. Thus G, which is a fifth above C at the twelve o'clock position, can be placed in the one o'clock position. Similarly, F, which is a fifth below C, can be placed at the eleven o'clock position. Or, stated alternatively, C in the twelve o'clock position is a fifth above its predecessor, which is F in the eleven o'clock position. In this way, we can complete the entries in the circle of fifths. To maintain a perfect fifth, we must check that all adjacent entries are seven half steps apart. This will soon necessitate the use of black as well as white keys.

FIGURE 2 – The Circle of Fifths

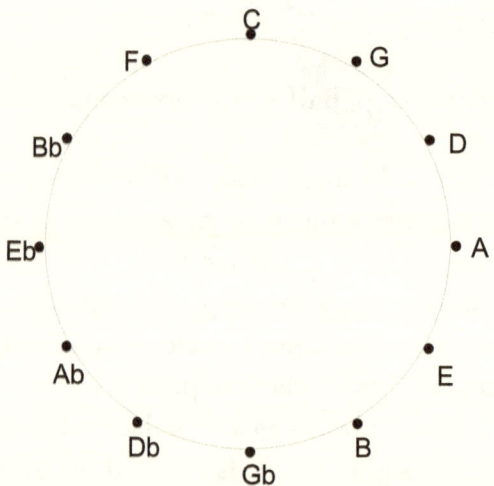

The letters on the circle of fifths represent more than notes, however. They represent *key notes*. Thus the twelve o'clock position refers not only to the single note C but also to the other seven notes of the C major scale and their various combinations. One of the most common of these combinations of notes in a key is the tonic triad, which is constructed from the first, third, and fifth notes of the corresponding scale. Thus, for the C scale of C, D, E, F, G, A, B, and C, the tonic triad is C + E+ G.

Examining the one o'clock position, G is the key note. The G major scale can be constructed by beginning on its key note and proceeding to the right with the same differences of half step and whole steps as in the C major scale. These were (whole step, whole step, half step), whole step, and (whole step, whole step, half step). Applying these relations to the key note G, we arrive at the G major scale, G, A, B, C, D, E, F♯ (read "F sharp"), and G. The sharp symbol (♯) is an instruction to substitute the named note, in this case F, with the note a half step above it. If we did not raise the F to F♯, the second half of our G scale would be D, E, F, G and would have the relation (whole step, half step, and whole step). This does not match the tetrachord pattern for a major scale, which is (whole tone, whole tone, half step). In order to correct this discrepancy and create a major scale, the F needs to be raised a half step to F♯. This alteration creates the key signature shown in Figure 3, which tells the musician that when the key note is G, all Fs must be raised and substituted by the black note F♯. Therefore, the circle of fifths can also be regarded as a circle of key signatures.

FIGURE 3

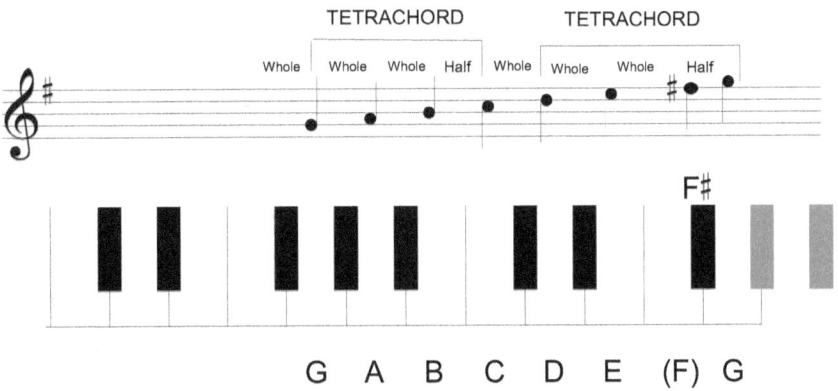

Turning to the eleven o'clock position, F is the key note. If we play the white keys from an F to the next F, the differences between the keys F, G, A, B, C, D, E, and F are whole step, whole step, whole step, half step, whole step, whole step, half. In this case, the second tetrachord of C + D + E + F has the correct relations for the major scale, while the first one, F+ G + A + B, does not. The notes F + G + A + B, with each note separated by a whole tone, form an interval called a tritone between F and B (also known as *diabolus* in music). For this tetrachord to conform to the pattern used in the major scale (whole tone, whole tone, half step) the B must be lowered to the black note a half step lower in pitch, B♭, read as "B flat." Just as a sharp (♯) tells us that a note should be raised by a half step, a flat (♭) tells us that it should be lowered by a half step. Thus, when F is the key note, the key signature shown in Figure 4 tells the performer that all Bs must be replaced by B♭, the black note just to the left of B.

FIGURE 4

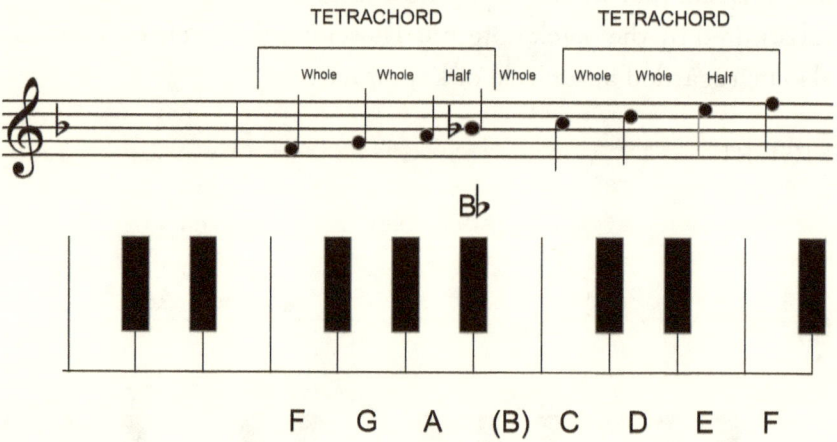

Through the same process, one can generate the scales of the remaining key notes. Each key note will have an associated key signature that tells the performer which named notes must be raised or lowered. By convention, the sharp (♯) keys are written on the right-hand side of the circle of fifths and tend to have brighter qualities, with the darker flat (♭) keys placed on the left. Each set of notes and harmonies associated with a different key center can evoke different qualities (such as brightness/darkness) when employed in a musical composition. The D major triad is brighter than that of A♭ major, for example. As a result, the choice of key and the exploitation of its intrinsic qualities by composers of classical music were critical to the success with which their compositions evoked the desired effect. The choice of key was also influenced by the physical capabilities and properties of the specific instruments employed, whether wind, brass, strings, or keyboard. The qualities of a specific key, like those of an individual personality, are multifaceted, incapable of reduction into few words, and subject to inter-observer variations, but there seems to be a general agreement regarding their dominant aspects. Prior to the late nineteenth century, the tuning of keyboard instruments in unequal temperaments tended to exaggerate the distinctive key qualities.

The German poet and musician Christian Schubart, a contemporary of Mozart, formulated a list of the different keys and the associated qualities each evokes. This list was published posthumously in 1806 in his *Ideen Zu Einer Äesthetik Der Tonkunst*. For our purposes, the following edited table was derived from his entries for the major keys. How the minor keys, whether tonic or relative, relate to the qualities of their major counterparts will not be discussed in this treatise.

Table 1

KEY	QUALITY
C major	Totally pure
G major	Every calm and gratified passion
D major	The key of triumph and war cries
A major	Satisfaction with one's position
E major	Laughing delight
B major	Declaring savage passion
G♭ major	Triumph in difficulty
D♭ major	A leering key

A♭ major	The key of the grave; eternity lies in its sphere
E♭ major	The key of love
B♭ major	Humorous affection
F major	Pleasure, calm

CHAPTER 2

The Zodiac and Planets for the Non-Astrologer

In the Springtime, seed is sown.
In the Summer, grass is mown.
In the Autumn, you may reap.
Winter is the time for sleep.

—W. S. Gilbert

The wheel of the zodiac first appeared in the ancient Middle East prior to 500 BC. This model for ordering the movement of the planets and tracking the seasons was subsequently adopted by the ancient Greek and Roman cultures. It then passed to the emerging modern Western European culture during the Renaissance. Western classical harmony was formalized during this same time period, emerging in its mature form at the beginning of the seventeenth century. In the search for the relationship between the astrological and musical mindsets and how the former may have affected the development of the latter, it is necessary to look at the understanding of the stars that existed during the beginning of the Renaissance. A brief summary of astrology circa AD 1400 is provided by the English poet John Gower in Book VII of his *Confessio Amantis*. Contemporaries of Gower, such as Geoffrey Chaucer, conflated the qualities associated with the planets with those of their associated mythological deities.

Gower describes the spheres around the Earth as given by Ptolemy in the geocentric model. The ascending spheres contain the moon, Mercury, Venus, sun, Mars, Jupiter, Saturn, and the stars. The outer sphere, in which the stars move, contains the twelve signs of the zodiac.

The moon, which "has to do with the sea" and travel, moves on the closest sphere. In Greek mythology, Diana was the moon goddess. She was a huntress and a virgin. In a famous myth, during a hunt, Actaeon accidentally stumbled upon Diana bathing naked. She punished him by transforming him into a stag, and he was pursued and killed by his own hounds. The mythological association with Diana thus confers on the moon the attributes of the hunt and purity.

Second above the moon lies Mercury. Gower describes its nature as studious and curious, loving ease and rest, and motivated by riches. In myth, the god Mercury was the fleet-footed messenger of Jupiter and also a cunning thief and trickster.

Next to Mercury stands the planet Venus, which "governs all the nations of lovers." Those born under Venus are "soft and sweet ... desiring joy and mirth." In myth, Venus is the goddess of love and beauty.

In the forth sphere moves the sun, which Gower describes as "the chief planet imperial, above him and beneath him three as he has the middle place among the seven." His aspect is of goodwill and liberality. In myth, Apollo is associated with the sun.

Mars, the "planet of battle, stands above the glorious Sun." Mars imparts a fierce disposition and a desire for war and strife. Mars is the god of war.

Jupiter moves in the sixth sphere and "causes peace and no debate." In myth, the god Jupiter is the supreme ruler and thrower of thunderbolts. He is also a libertine whose uncontrolled passions involve him in many infidelities, during which he often transforms himself into wild beasts.

"Highest and above all stands the planet Saturn, whose complexion is cold, and whose condition causes malice and cruelty." In mythology, Saturn once ruled heaven, but he was deposed and banished by his son Jupiter. This change of fortune probably contributed to his bitter malevolence.

Gower's poem continues with the description of the signs of the zodiac, which move in the starry sphere. He names them in order and gives the months and planets that are associated with them. Table 2 lists the planets, their associated astrologic and mythological attributes, and the signs that they rule.

Table 2

Planet Signs	Quality	Ruling
moon	The sea, travel, the hunt, and purity (Diana)	Cancer (the Crab)
Mercury	Studious, curious, lazy Fleet-footed, cunning trickster (myth)	Gemini (the Twins) Virgo (the Maiden)
Venus	Love and beauty	Taurus (the Bull) Libra (the Scales)
sun	Imperial	Leo (the Lion)
Mars	War and struggle	Aries (the Ram) Scorpio (the Scorpion)
Jupiter	Peace Uncontrolled passion (myth)	Sagittarius (the Monstrous Archer) Pisces (the Fish)
Saturn	Cold, malicious, and cruel	Capricorn (the Goat) Aquarius (the Water Bearer)

CHAPTER 3

Using Qualities to Match Key Notes to the Planets

From the material in Chapters 1 and 2, Table 3 can be constructed.

Table 3

Planet	Quality	Key Note
moon	Pure (Diana)	C
Mercury	Humorous affection (trickster)	B♭
	Laughing delight (trickster)	E
Venus	Love	E♭
	Gratified passion	G
sun	Satisfaction with one's position (Imperial)	A
Mars	War cries	D
	Triumph	F♯ (G♭)
Jupiter	Pleasure, calm (peace)	F
	Savage passion (libertine)	B
Saturn	Leering (malicious, cruel)	D♭
	The grave (cold)	A♭

Because the goal of this book is to relate the twelve points on the wheel of the zodiac to those on the circle of fifths, only one key note was given to the luminaries, the sun and moon, because they each rule only one sign of the zodiac. The other five planets can be divided into types based on the interval between their associated notes. Venus and Mars are each defined by a major third, with Venus's two notes a clashing half tone above those of Mars, perhaps reflecting the eternal struggle between love and war. Jupiter and Mercury are defined by tritones, perhaps representing the unstable nature of the master and his servant. It is of interest that Mercury's key notes are the same as those employed in the corresponding movement from Holst's suite *The Planets*. Saturn stands appropriately alone, defined by a perfect fifth made up of two black keys. Saturn is thus banished from the white keys and is the only planet that has no representative among them.

Simple chords are formed by the combination of planets by elemental type as given by Gower and others. The C minor triad is formed by the moon with Venus, the cold and wet planets representing the element water and the phlegmatic temperament. The D major triad is formed by the sun and Mars, the hot and dry planets representing fire and the choleric. Saturn, cold and dry and representing the element earth and the melancholic, combines with Jupiter, hot and wet and representing air and the sanguine, to produce a Db7 chord. Mercury remains ethereal and undefined in this schema.

It is possible to create a circle of the planets by pairing the different planet types with the masculine on the left and the female on the right. Mercury is hermaphroditic and will be considered female in this scheme. The unpaired Saturn will be placed at the top.

Figure 5 The Circle of Planets

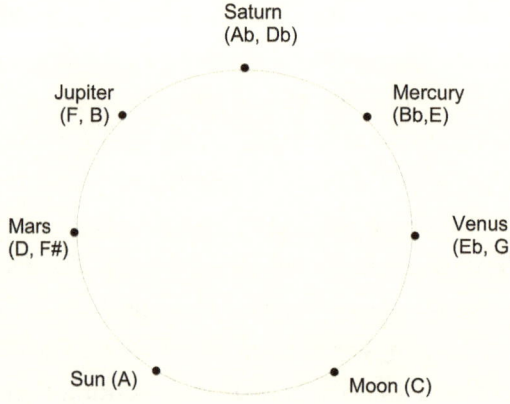

It is also possible to plot the scales and chords derived from various intervals on this circle. These include the chromatic scale in half steps, the two whole-tone scales (in whole steps), diminished seventh chords based on the minor third, augmented triads based on the major third, tritone pairs, and the circle of fifths. All these diagrams produce symmetrical patterns.

Chromatic Scale

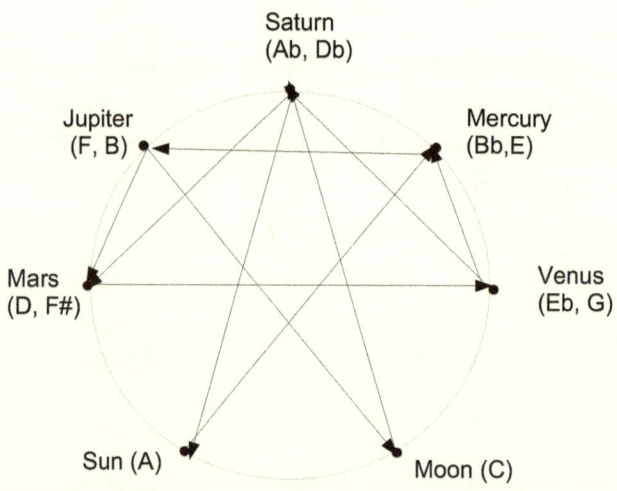

Two Whole-tone Scales

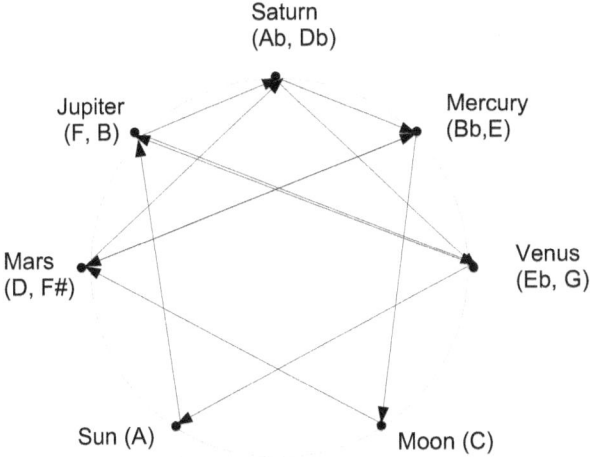

Three Diminished Seventh Chords Based on Minor Thirds

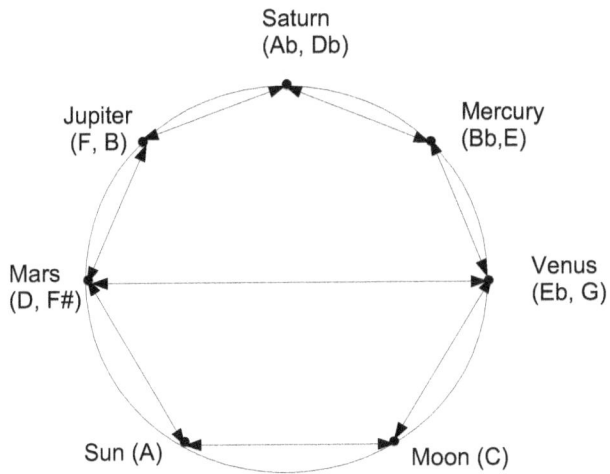

The simplicity of this pattern and its largely peripheral location on the circle attests to the fact that the three diminished seventh chords occupy distinct, non-overlapping regions of the circle.

Four Augmented Triads Based on Major Thirds

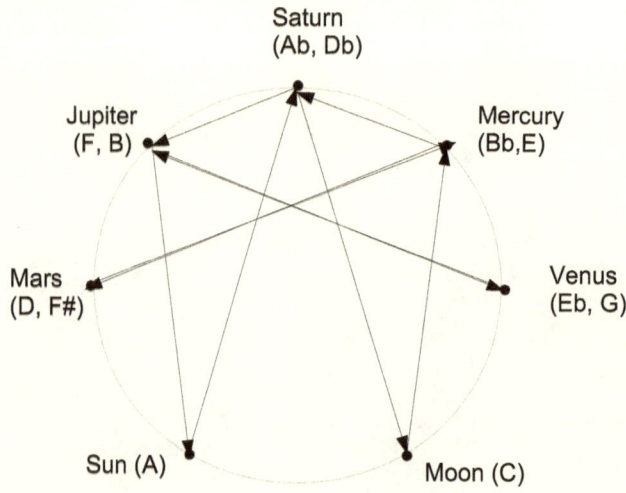

Six Tritone Pairs

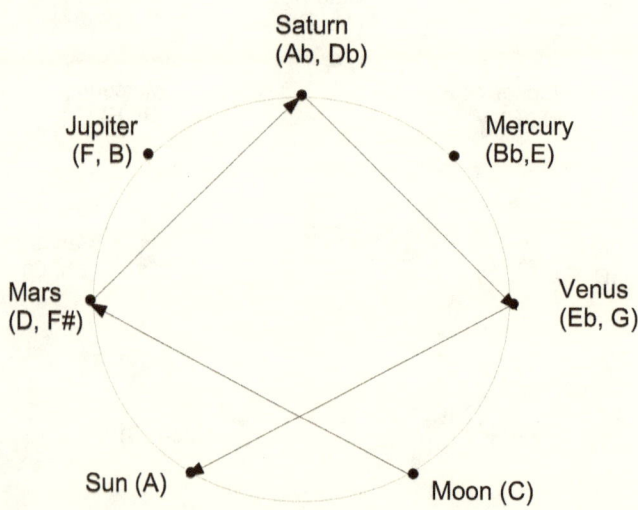

As previously stated, the key notes of Jupiter and Mercury are both tritone pairs.

Circle of Fifths

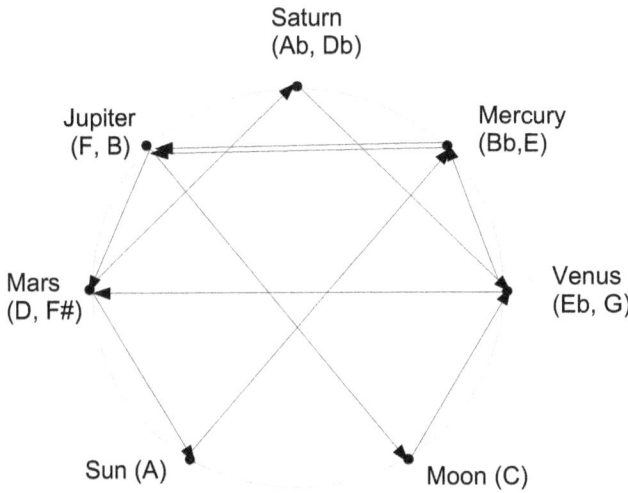

Thus, all scales and chords based on a single interval create symmetrical patterns when plotted on the circle of planets.

Planets on the Circle of Fifths

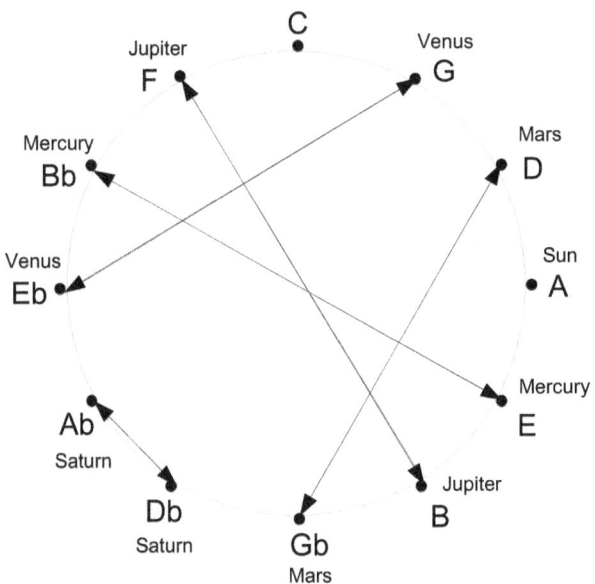

CHAPTER 4

Relating the Twelve Key Notes of the Circle of Fifths to the Twelve Signs on the Wheel of the Zodiac

We now proceed to assign specific key notes to the signs of the zodiac. Combining the information in Table 2 and Table 3, we obtain the following results plotted on the wheel of the zodiac.

Figure 6 – Planets and Key Notes Plotted on the Wheel of the Zodiac

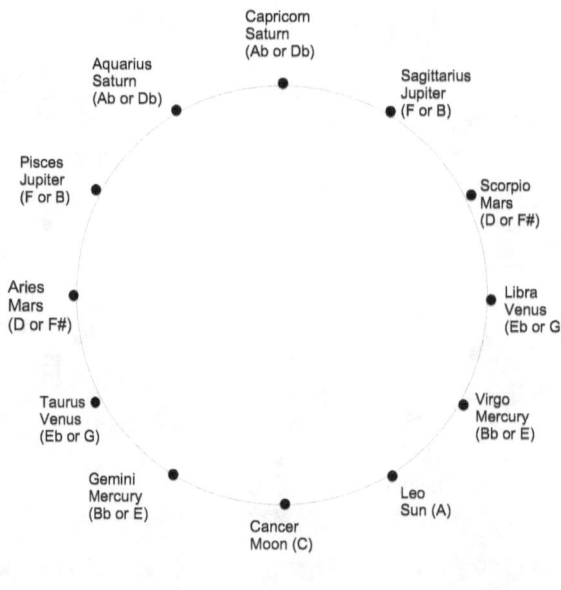

If we eliminate the planet names from the diagram and choose key notes by the convention of brighter, sharp keys to the right and darker, flat keys to the left, we obtain the following configuration.

Figure 7

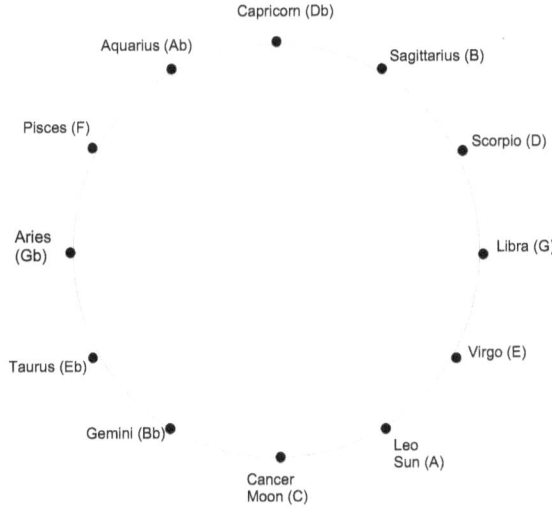

We have placed the brighter, sharp keys on the sun side of the wheel and the darker keys on the moon side. In the Aries position, the F♯ was replaced by its enharmonic G♭. The choice of D♭ for Capricorn (rather than A♭) was undertaken to rise a whole step from the B at Sagittarius. In this way the whole-step transition from autumn to winter mirrors that of spring to summer—the whole step from the B♭ of Gemini to the C of Cancer.

The notes assigned to the signs of the zodiac, when ordered sequentially, create a tone row that can be written as follows, with the triads that are formed within each corresponding three-month season.

G♭, E♭, B♭	C, A, E	G, D, B	and	D♭, A♭, F
E♭ minor	A minor	G major	and	D♭ major
spring	summer	autumn	and	winter

As with the circle of planets, we can now plot the various scales, chords, and patterns generated by half steps, whole steps, minor and major thirds, tritones, and fifths onto the annotated wheel of the zodiac, checking for symmetry and comparing the figures to the same musical structures plotted on the circle of fifths.

Chromatic Scale on the Wheel of the Zodiac

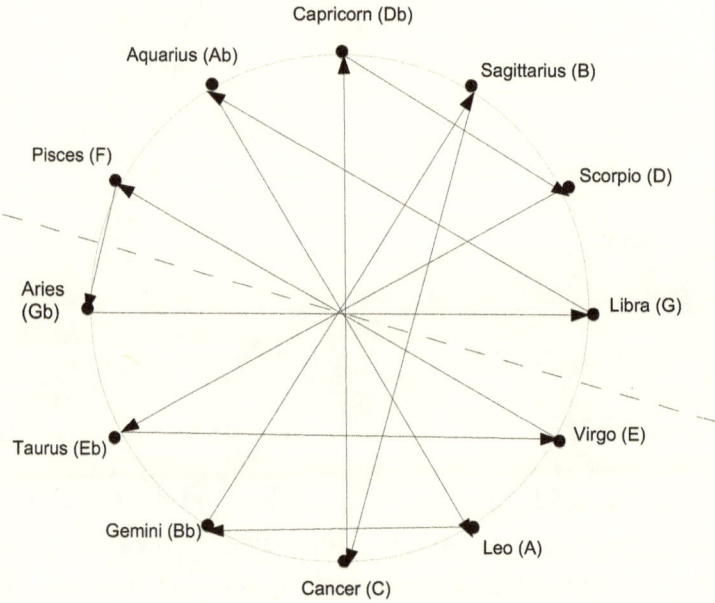

This figure is symmetric around the dashed line that separates the signs of spring and summer from those of autumn and winter.

The Chromatic Scale on the Circle of Fifths

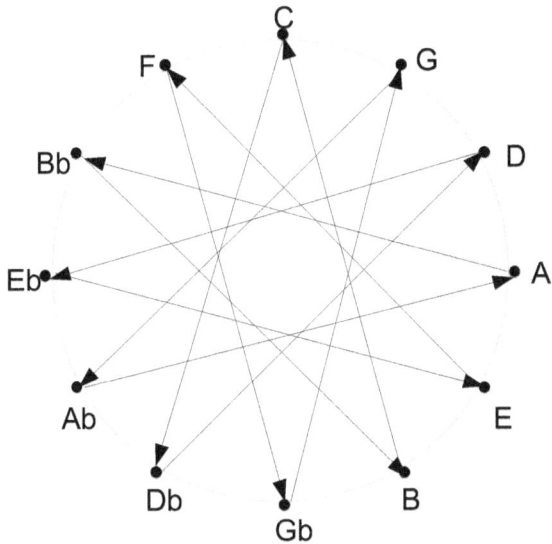

The Two Whole-tone Scales on the Wheel of the Zodiac

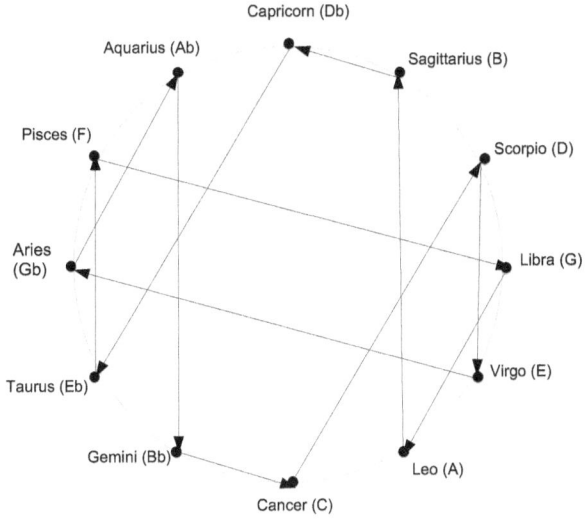

This diagram and its symmetry inform us of a simple way that the notes of the twelve signs can be remembered.

Beginning at Aries, write the whole-tone scale, starting on G♭. Beginning at Libra, write the whole-tone scale, starting on G. This gives the following configuration.

G♭, A♭, B♭,	C, D, E,	G, A, B,	D♭, E♭, F
spring	summer	autumn	winter

We then exchange the middle entry of winter and spring; that is, we switch the positions of A♭ and E♭ and do the same for summer and autumn—meaning that we switch the positions of A and D. In this way, we arrive at the same tone row obtained previously by matching qualities of key notes and planets and assigning them to the wheel of the zodiac as demonstrated.

G♭, E♭, B♭	C, A, E,	G, D, B,	D♭, A♭, F

The Two Whole-tone Scales on the Circle of Fifths

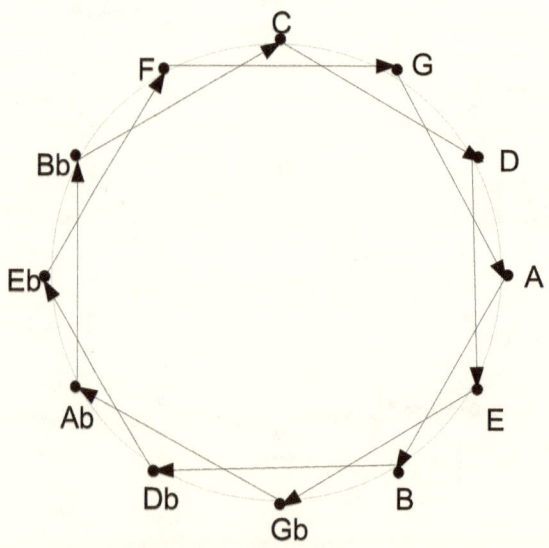

The Three Diminished Seventh Chords on the Wheel of the Zodiac

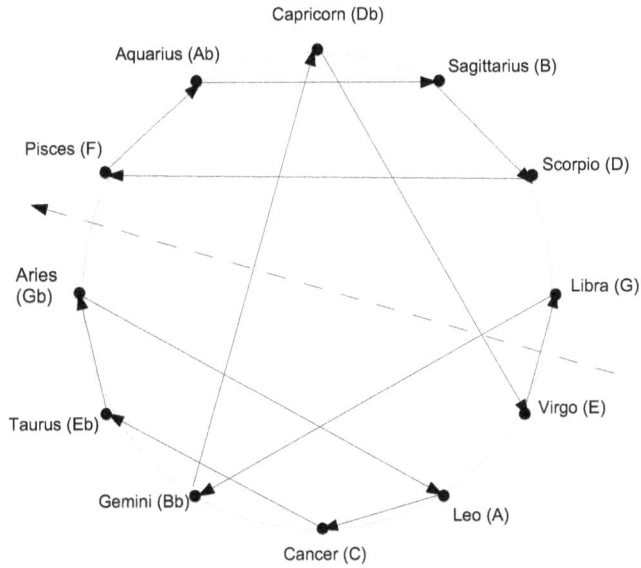

The Diminished Seventh Chords on the Circle of Fifths

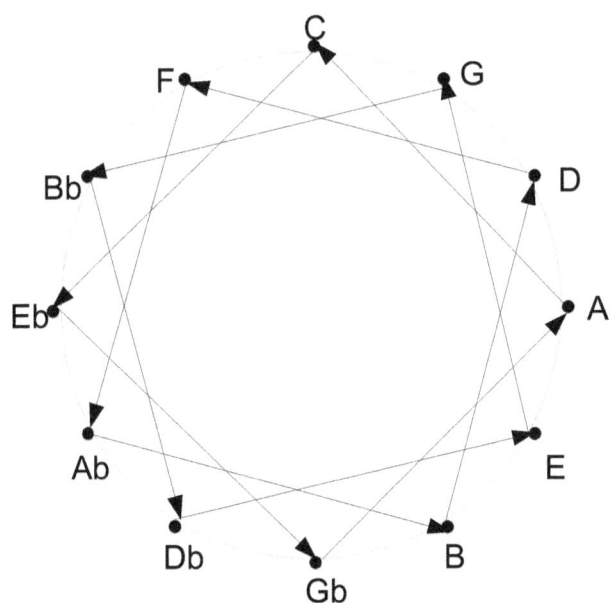

The Four Augmented Triads on the Wheel of the Zodiac

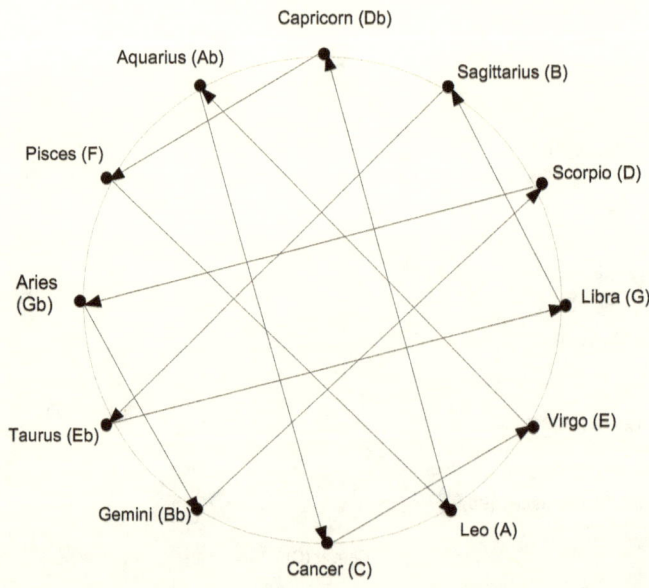

The Four Augmented Triads on the Circle of Fifths

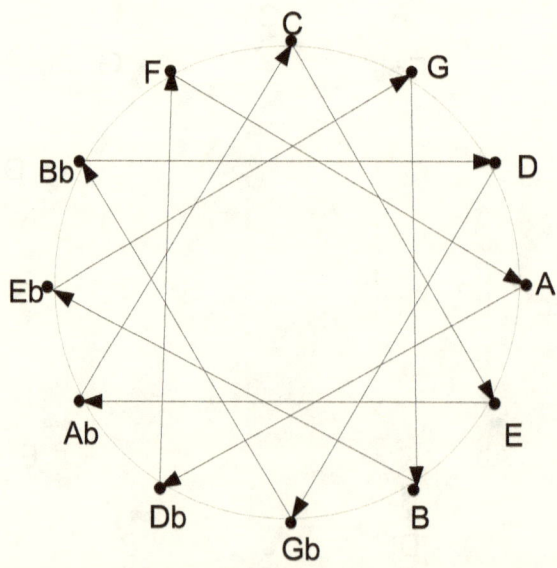

Six Tritone Pairs on the Wheel of the Zodiac

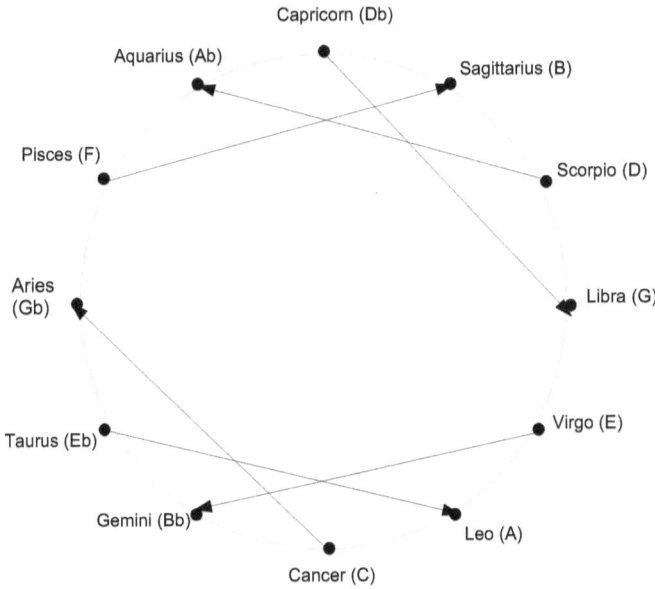

Six Tritone Pairs on the Circle of Fifths

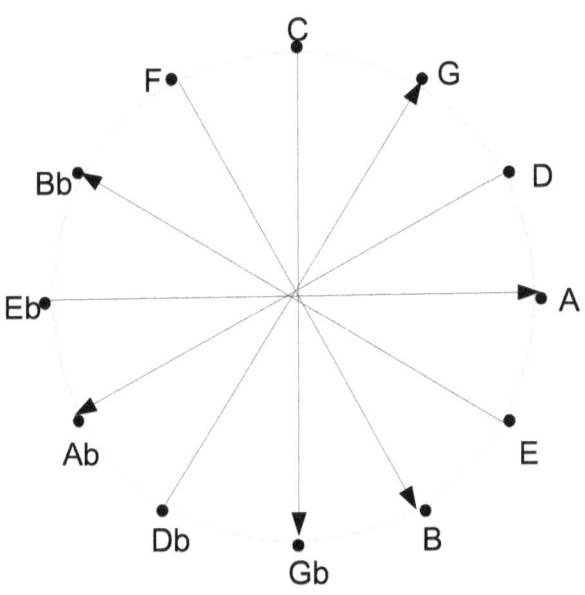

The Circle of Fifths on the Wheel of the Zodiac

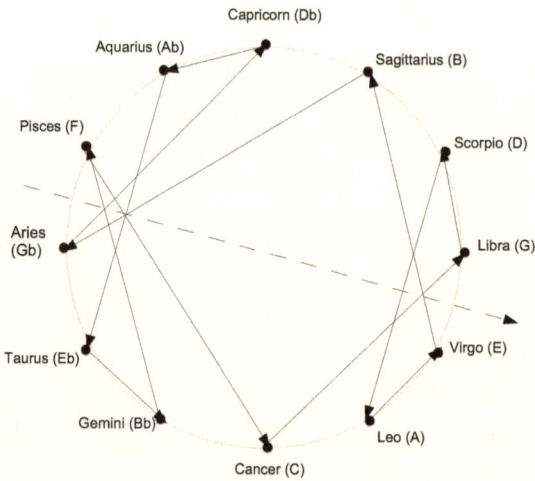

Thus, all scales and chords based on a single interval create symmetrical patterns when plotted on the annotated wheel of the zodiac.

Now observe the wheel of the zodiac on the circle of fifths. When the tone row based on the key notes of the signs of the zodiac is plotted sequentially from Aries through Pisces on the circle of fifths, once again a symmetrical pattern emerges.

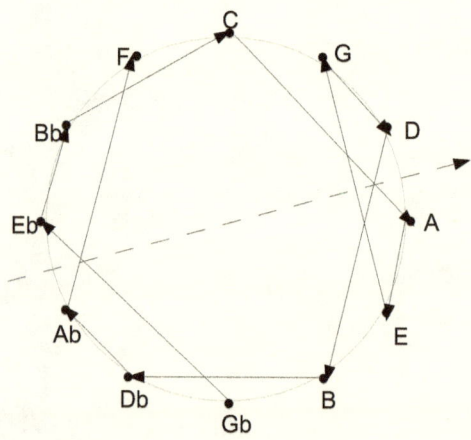

CHAPTER 5

Musical Examples

When the notes associated with the planets are sounded in the order of their associated days of the week, they form the following sequences (bars 1–12).

By playing the notes of the planets in ascending order according to the Ptolemaic model, we obtain another sequence (bars 13–16). This can be analyzed harmonically as C major for three beats, E♭ major for three, D major for four beats, and D♭7 for four beats. Alternatively, all key notes can be stacked vertically, creating a polytonal effect (bars 17–23).

From the tone row of keys associated with the signs of the zodiac played in sequence from Aries to Pisces, the music of bar 24–31 is derived.

Days of the Week

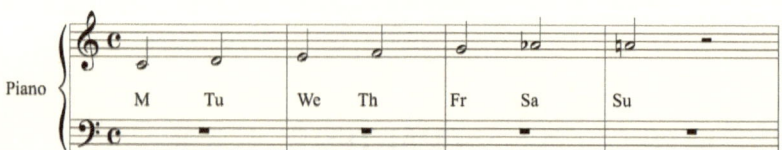

Shadow Scale

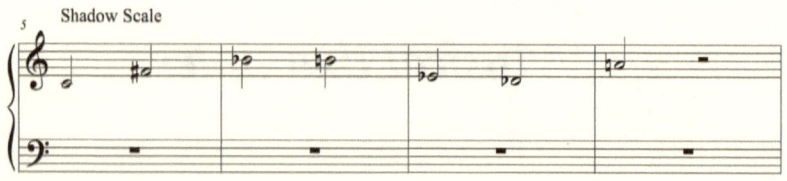

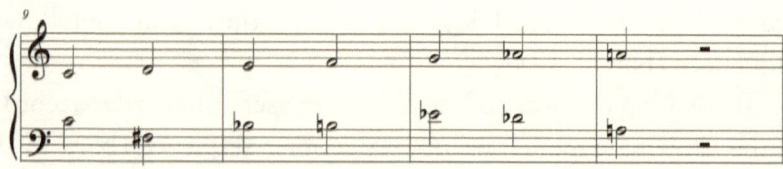

Planetary Sequences

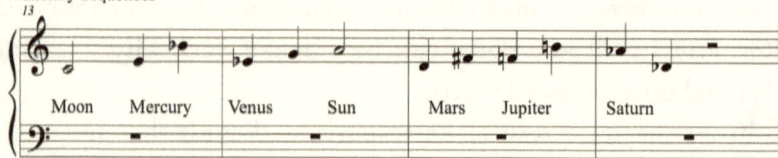

Passing
of Seasons

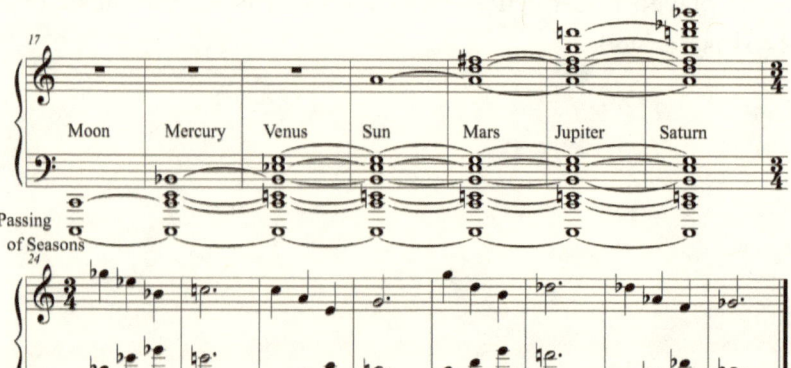

ABOUT THE AUTHOR

Michael Bank, a professional jazz pianist and composer since 1988, studied stride piano, harmony, and composition with master musician Jaki Byard. A graduate of Harvard College, he received his medical degree from the Columbia College of Physicians and Surgeons. He currently practices medicine in upstate New York. He can be reached at michael@michaelbank.com.

www.ingramcontent.com/pod-product-compliance
Lightning Source LLC
Chambersburg PA
CBHW021850170526
45157CB00006B/2386